THIS BOOK BELONGS TO:

_____

_____

Shop our other books at
www.sillyslothpress.com

For questions and customer service, email us at
support@sillyslothpress.com

WOULD YOU RATHER...

...NOT TALK ALL DAY OR NOT PLAY ALL DAY?

WOULD YOU RATHER...

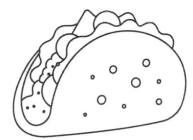

...EAT A TACO WITHOUT MEAT OR WITHOUT CHEESE?

WOULD YOU RATHER...

...BE STRANDED ON A DESERT ISLAND
OR
BE STRANDED IN THE RAINFOREST?

WOULD YOU RATHER...

...BE SNEEZED ON BY SOMEONE
OR
HAVE SOMEONE PICK YOUR NOSE?

WOULD YOU RATHER...

...USE LEAVES FOR TOILET PAPER OR MAYONNAISE FOR SHAMPOO?

WOULD YOU RATHER...

...HAVE A THIRD EYE OR A THIRD ARM?

WOULD YOU RATHER...

...HAVE GUM THAT NEVER LOSES FLAVOR OR A LOLLIPOP THAT LASTS FOREVER?

WOULD YOU RATHER...

...SMELL FARTS FOR MONEY OR GET PAID TO SMELL STINKY FEET?

WOULD YOU RATHER...

...EAT YOUR OWN POOP ONCE A DAY OR DRINK YOUR PEE WITH EVERY MEAL?

WOULD YOU RATHER...

...BE THE TOOTH FAIRY OR THE EASTER BUNNY?

WOULD YOU RATHER...

...HAVE TO SNIFF YOUR FRIEND'S FEET OR HAVE YOUR FRIEND SNIFF YOUR FEET?

WOULD YOU RATHER...

...HAVE A HEAD THE SIZE OF A LEMON OR THE SIZE OF A PUMPKIN?

WOULD YOU RATHER...

...HAVE EVERYONE FORGET ABOUT YOUR BIRTHDAY OR YOU FORGET ABOUT EVERYONE ELSE'S BIRTHDAY?

WOULD YOU RATHER...

...SWIM IN SHARK INFESTED WATERS OR JUMP FREE FALL WITH A PARACHUTE INTO THE GRAND CANYON?

WOULD YOU RATHER...

...HAVE EARWAX FLAVORED ICE CREAM OR ICE CREAM FLAVORED EARWAX?

WOULD YOU RATHER...

...HAVE 100 SIBLINGS OR 100 PETS?

WOULD YOU RATHER...

...HAVE A BACK
MASSAGE
WITH SNOT
OR
ROTTEN EELS?

WOULD YOU RATHER...

...STAY UP ALL
NIGHT WATCHING
CARTOONS
OR
SKIP A DAY
OF SCHOOL?

WOULD YOU RATHER...

...POOP CANDY
OR
PEE
LEMONADE?

WOULD YOU RATHER...

...WALK BAREFOOT
THROUGH
ELEPHANT
POOP
OR
THROUGH POISON IVY?

WOULD YOU RATHER...

...HAVE YOUR BREATH SMELL LIKE FART OR HAVE YOUR LAUGH SOUND LIKE A FART?

WOULD YOU RATHER...

...VISIT A GOOD AMUSEMENT PARK ONCE A MONTH OR GO TO THE BEST AMUSEMENT PARK ONCE EVERY YEAR?

WOULD YOU RATHER...

...WEAR UNDERWEAR THAT IS TOO TIGHT
OR
SHOES THAT ARE TOO SMALL?

WOULD YOU RATHER...

...HAVE
A SUBMARINE
OR
A SPACESHIP?

WOULD YOU RATHER...

...HAVE TO ANNOUNCE EVERY TIME YOU HAVE TO PEE
OR
EVERY TIME YOU HAVE TO FART?

WOULD YOU RATHER...

...HAVE A MAGIC BUTTON THAT MAKES YOUR PARENTS STOP TALKING
OR
A MAGIC BUTTON THAT MAKES YOUR TEACHER STOP TALKING?

WOULD YOU RATHER...

...GET CAUGHT EATING A BOOGER OR PICKING A WEDGIE?

WOULD YOU RATHER...

...EXPLORE A CAVE OR AN IGLOO?

WOULD YOU RATHER...

...BE CHASED BY A ZOMBIE OR BE HAUNTED BY A GHOST?

WOULD YOU RATHER...

...GET STUNG BY A JELLYFISH OR PINCHED BY A CRAB?

WOULD YOU RATHER...

...YOUR ENTIRE HOUSE BE AS BOUNCY AS A TRAMPOLINE OR SINK IN LIKE QUICKSAND?

WOULD YOU RATHER...

...HAVE A TIME MACHINE OR A SPACESHIP?

WOULD YOU RATHER...

...HAVE A FLYING MAGIC CARPET
OR
AN INVISIBILITY CLOAK?

WOULD YOU RATHER...

...HAVE A NOSE THAT GROWS WHEN YOU LIE
OR
EARS THAT GROW WHEN YOU GET ANGRY?

...THROW UP
OR
FART SUPER LOUDLY
IN FRONT OF YOUR
CLASSMATES?

...HAVE DANDRUFF
MADE OF SUGAR
OR
POOP MADE
OF BIRTHDAY CAKE?

WOULD YOU RATHER...

...DRINK HOT SODA OR EAT A COLD HAMBURGER?

WOULD YOU RATHER...

...HAVE TO SHED YOUR SKIN LIKE A SNAKE OR LAY EGGS LIKE A CHICKEN?

...RAISE CHICKENS FOR THEIR EGGS OR COWS FOR THEIR MILK?

...NEVER LISTEN TO MUSIC OR NEVER WATCH TV?

WOULD YOU RATHER...

...EXPLORE THE MOON OR DISCOVER A BURIED TREASURE ON EARTH?

WOULD YOU RATHER...

...HAVE TOES INSTEAD OF FINGERS OR FINGERS INSTEAD OF TOES?

WOULD YOU RATHER...

...ALWAYS DRINK YOUR FOOD FROM A BABY BOTTLE OR ALWAYS WEAR DIAPERS?

WOULD YOU RATHER...

...HAVE HOTDOGS FOR FINGERS OR BANANAS FOR TOES?

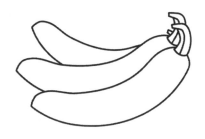

WOULD YOU RATHER...

...HAVE A TREEHOUSE
OR
AN UNDERGROUND
HIDEOUT?

WOULD YOU RATHER...

...EAT A STICK
OF BUTTER
OR
A BOTTLE
OF MUSTARD?

...WEAR
A WITCH HAT
TO SCHOOL
OR
A PIRATE PATCH?

...BE ABLE TO WALK
THROUGH WALLS
OR
SEE THROUGH
WALLS?

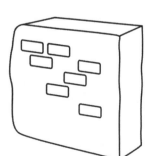

WOULD YOU RATHER...

...NEVER EAT DESSERT OR NEVER SLEEP?

WOULD YOU RATHER...

...HAVE TO TAKE ONE BITE OF THE STINKIEST CHEESE OR EAT A FRESH SNAIL FROM THE OCEAN?

WOULD YOU RATHER...

...MOO LIKE A COW EVERY TIME YOU LAUGH OR GOBBLE LIKE A TURKEY EVERY TIME YOU SCREAM?

WOULD YOU RATHER...

...LICK A DUMPSTER OR EAT MOLDY BACON?

WOULD YOU RATHER...

...HAVE A CONSTANT WEDGIE OR AN AWFUL HAIRCUT WHEREVER YOU GO?

WOULD YOU RATHER...

...RIDE A FARTING HORSE OR KISS A BURPING FROG?

...BE A SUPERHERO THAT NO ONE KNOWS OR BE A SUPER VILLAIN THAT EVERYONE KNOWS?

...HAVE THE DIET OF AN ANTEATER OR THE DIET OF A WORM?

WOULD YOU RATHER...

...EAT EGGS THAT FEEL SLIMY OR EGGS THAT SMELL ROTTEN?

WOULD YOU RATHER...

...SIT IN AN ANT PILE OR HAVE FLEAS CRAWLING ALL OVER YOUR BODY?

WOULD YOU RATHER...

...SEE PLANTS GROW
12 TIMES LARGER
OR
SEE ANIMALS
SHRINK
12 TIMES SMALLER?

WOULD YOU RATHER...

...STAY HOME FOR
A MONTH STRAIGHT
OR
STAY AT SCHOOL
WITH YOUR FRIENDS
AND TEACHERS
FOR A MONTH STRAIGHT?

WOULD YOU RATHER...

...CATCH A LEPRECHAUN OR SEE SANTA ON CHRISTMAS EVE?

WOULD YOU RATHER...

...HAVE A CAT SIZED ELEPHANT OR A MOUSE SIZED GOAT?

WOULD YOU RATHER...

...RIDE A FLYING BUS
OR
RIDE
A UNICORN?

WOULD YOU RATHER...

...SPEND A NIGHT
IN A HAUNTED
CASTLE
OR
AN UNDERWATER
HOTEL?

WOULD YOU RATHER...

...MEET YOUR FAVORITE BOOK CHARACTER
OR
SOMEONE FAMOUS FROM HISTORY?

WOULD YOU RATHER...

...BE AN INCREDIBLE ARTIST
OR
AN AMAZING DANCER?

WOULD YOU RATHER...

...EAT PIZZA
FOR BREAKFAST
EVERY MORNING
OR
WAFFLES FOR DINNER
EVERY EVENING?

WOULD YOU RATHER...

...HOP LIKE
A KANGAROO
OR
WALK LIKE
A TURTLE?

WOULD YOU RATHER...

...ACE A MATH TEST OR AN ENGLISH TEST?

WOULD YOU RATHER...

...BE THE SMARTEST KID AT SCHOOL OR THE FASTEST RUNNER AT SCHOOL?

WOULD YOU RATHER...

...LIVE WITH AN ALIEN FAMILY IN OUTER SPACE OR WITH A FAMILY OF HIPPOS?

WOULD YOU RATHER...

...HAVE TO EAT WITH YOUR FEET OR WALK WITH YOUR HANDS?

WOULD YOU RATHER...

...HOLD A CENTIPEDE
OR
LICK
AN OCTOPUS?

WOULD YOU RATHER...

...NEVER HAVE
TO DO CHORES
OR
NEVER HAVE
TO GO TO SCHOOL
FOR THE REST
OF YOUR LIFE?

WOULD YOU RATHER...

...HAVE EYEBROWS THAT NEVER STOPPED GROWING
OR
HAVE NO EYEBROWS AT ALL?

WOULD YOU RATHER...

...SPEND A DAY AT THE ZOO
OR
A DAY AT THE BEACH?

...BE A DOCTOR FOR PEOPLE OR A VETERINARIAN?

...HAVE A FOOD FIGHT OR A WATER BALLOON FIGHT?

...BE A TEACHER'S PET
OR
A CLASS
CLOWN?

...NEVER GET SICK AGAIN
OR
NEVER HAVE TO TAKE
ANOTHER TEST
IN SCHOOL?

WOULD YOU RATHER...

...SNEEZE 30 MOTHS OR COUGH UP A GERBIL?

WOULD YOU RATHER...

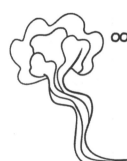

...SHARE A ROOM WITH SOMEONE WHO SNORES OR SOMEONE WHO FARTS IN THEIR SLEEP?

...ALWAYS HAVE WET SOCKS OR ALWAYS HAVE SHOES THAT SMELL LIKE HORSE POOP?

...HAVE THE TAIL OF A PIG OR THE FIN OF A SHARK?

...TRAVEL BY PLANE OR TRAVEL BY HOT AIR BALLOON?

...BE A VENTRILOQUIST OR COMMUNICATE WITH YOUR MIND?

WOULD YOU RATHER...

...HAVE SILENT FARTS THAT SMELL AWFUL OR LOUD FARTS THAT DON'T STINK?

WOULD YOU RATHER...

...HAVE ANGEL WINGS OR A MERMAID TAIL?

WOULD YOU RATHER...

...PICK YOUR FRIEND'S NOSE OR WIPE YOUR FRIEND'S BUTT?

WOULD YOU RATHER...

...BE LICKED BY 10 DROOLING PUPPIES OR BE SAT ON BY ONE LARGE DOG?

WOULD YOU RATHER...

...LIVE WITHOUT ICE CREAM OR WITHOUT CANDY?

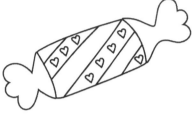

WOULD YOU RATHER...

...BE BITTEN BY A VAMPIRE OR A ZOMBIE?

WOULD YOU RATHER...

...HAVE THE POWER TO BE INVISIBLE OR THE ABILITY TO TALK TO ANIMALS?

WOULD YOU RATHER...

...TAKE A BATH IN ICE OR JELLO?

...PICK SOMEONE'S
EARWAX
OR
CLIP SOMEONE'S
DIRTY TOENAILS?

...SLEEP IN A
NEST MADE
FROM DOG FUR
OR
HUMAN HAIR?

WOULD YOU RATHER...

...HAVE TO DANCE EVERYWHERE YOU GO

OR

SING EVERY TIME YOU SPEAK?

WOULD YOU RATHER...

...HAVE TO FIGHT 100 PIGEON SIZED ZEBRAS

OR

ONE ZEBRA SIZED PIGEON?

...HAVE 2 BLIND EYES
OR
ONE CYCLOPS
EYE WITH GREAT
VISION?

...SEE SANTA COME DOWN
THE CHIMNEY
OR
WAKE UP TO THE
MOST PRESENTS
YOU'VE EVER HAD?

...LIVE AS
AN ANIMATED
CARTOON
CHARACTER
OR
LIVE AS AN ACTION
FIGURE TOY?

...SWIM IN A POOL
OF MARSHMALLOWS
OR
SWIM IN A POOL
OF CHOCOLATE?

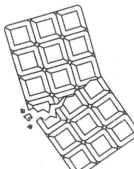

WOULD YOU RATHER...

...HAVE BAD BREATH OR ITCHY FEET?

WOULD YOU RATHER...

...GET ONE BEE STING OR 10 MOSQUITO BITES?

WOULD YOU RATHER...

...SLIDE DOWN A RAINBOW
OR
FIND A POT OF GOLD AT THE END OF A RAINBOW?

WOULD YOU RATHER...

...LIVE IN A TREEHOUSE
OR
A BOAT HOUSE?

...HAVE A MILLION DOLLARS OR A MILLION FRIENDS?

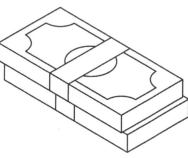

...HAVE HUGE MUSCLES BUT CAN ONLY LIFT 10LBS OR HAVE TINY MUSCLES BUT CAN LIFT 500LBS?

WOULD YOU RATHER...

...BE FAMOUS FOR DRAWING OR FAMOUS FOR SINGING?

WOULD YOU RATHER...

...SLEEP HANGING UPSIDE DOWN OR SLEEP IN A PILE OF DIRTY DIAPERS?

WOULD YOU RATHER...

...ONLY EAT FOODS THAT LOOK LIKE VOMIT
OR
FOODS THAT SMELL LIKE VOMIT?

WOULD YOU RATHER...

...WAKE UP WITH POOP IN YOUR PANTS EVERY DAY
OR PEE YOUR PANTS EVERY DAY AT SCHOOL?

...HAVE
20 FINGERS
OR
20 TOES?

...PLAY INSIDE
ALL DAY
OR
PLAY OUTSIDE
ALL DAY?

WOULD YOU RATHER...

...HAVE A PET DINOSAUR OR A PET UNICORN?

WOULD YOU RATHER...

...BE A NINJA OR KNOW EVERYONE'S SECRETS?

...EAT A BOWL OF SLUGS OR EAT A SINGLE SPIDER?

...DISCOVER A LIVING DINOSAUR OR A DRAGON EGG?

WOULD YOU RATHER...

...WALK ON YOUR HANDS OR ROLL LIKE A BALL TO GET AROUND?

WOULD YOU RATHER...

...HAVE UNLIMITED FOOD OR UNLIMITED TOYS?

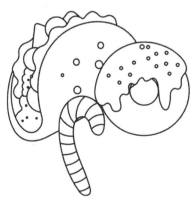

...SHARE YOUR BEDROOM WITH A TIGER OR 200 TARANTULAS?

...GET TRAPPED IN QUICKSAND OR IN THE BOOGERS OF A GIANT?

...MEET AN ALIEN OR TURN INTO A MERMAID?

...USE A PUBLIC TOILET WITH POOP ON THE SEAT OR ONE WITH A SNAKE IN IT?

WOULD YOU RATHER...

...WEAR
A CLOWN WIG
OR
A CLOWN
NOSE
EVERY DAY?

WOULD YOU RATHER...

...BE TRAPPED
IN AN ELEVATOR
WITH 5 WET
SLOTHS
OR
10 PEOPLE WITH
BAD BREATH?

...HAVE SUPER SPEED OR SUPER STRENGTH?

...BE AS TINY AS AN ANT OR AS BIG AS A WHALE?

WOULD YOU RATHER...

...BE THE FUNNIEST PERSON ALIVE
OR
THE SMARTEST PERSON ALIVE?

WOULD YOU RATHER...

...BE TOTALLY BALD OR COVERED FROM HEAD TO TOE WITH HAIR?

...HAVE 100 SPIDERS IN YOUR BEDROOM OR 1000 CRICKETS IN THE REST OF THE HOUSE?

...BE AN ONLY CHILD OR HAVE A TWIN?

...HAVE A PET RAT OR A PET SPIDER?

...EAT PIG FEET OR HAVE YOUR FEET LOOK LIKE PIG FEET?

...BUILD
A TOWER
OR
KNOCK
IT DOWN?

...HAVE
A HORSE'S TAIL
OR
A UNICORN
HORN?

WOULD YOU RATHER...

...NEVER HAVE HOMEWORK AGAIN OR BE PAID TO DO YOUR HOMEWORK?

WOULD YOU RATHER...

...HAVE A BABOON'S BUTT OR A GIRAFFE'S NECK?

WOULD YOU RATHER...

...LIVE IN AN AMUSEMENT PARK OR A ZOO?

WOULD YOU RATHER...

...SLEEP IN A BED FULL OF SAND OR CHOCOLATE SYRUP?

WOULD YOU RATHER...

...HAVE 100 COCKROACHES IN YOUR ROOM
OR
HAVE TO EAT ONE LIVE COCKROACH?

WOULD YOU RATHER...

...HAVE
ONE BEST FRIEND
OR
10 GOOD FRIENDS?

WOULD YOU RATHER...

...IT RAIN PEE OR SNOW POOP?

WOULD YOU RATHER...

...WAKE UP SUPER EARLY OR STAY UP SUPER LATE?

WOULD YOU RATHER...

...GROOM A CAT WITH YOUR TONGUE OR BE SPRAYED BY A SKUNK?

WOULD YOU RATHER...

...LIVE WAY DOWN IN THE SEA OR UP IN THE CLOUDS?

WOULD YOU RATHER...

...SET THE TABLE BEFORE DINNER
OR
WASH THE DISHES AFTER DINNER?

WOULD YOU RATHER...

...BE ABLE TO ONLY SMELL FARTS
OR
NEVER BE ABLE TO SMELL AGAIN?

WOULD YOU RATHER...

...HAVE A CARROT NOSE
LIKE A SNOWMAN
OR
A RED NOSE LIKE
RUDOLPH
THE RED-NOSED REINDEER?

WOULD YOU RATHER...

...GO FISHING
OR
HIKING?

WOULD YOU RATHER...

...EAT MELTED ICE CREAM OR COLD MACARONI?

WOULD YOU RATHER...

...HAVE HAIR MADE OF SQUID TENTACLES OR HAIR MADE OF CATERPILLARS?

WOULD YOU RATHER...

...BE ABLE TO FLY OR READ MINDS?

WOULD YOU RATHER...

...BE RAISED BY SLOTHS OR DONKEYS?

WOULD YOU RATHER...

...IT ALWAYS BE SUMMER OR ALWAYS BE WINTER?

WOULD YOU RATHER...

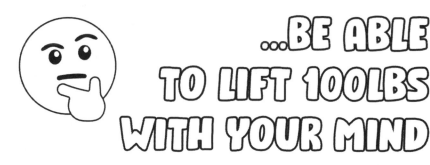

...BE ABLE TO LIFT 100LBS WITH YOUR MIND OR LIFT UP TO 10,000LBS WITH YOUR MUSCLES?

WOULD YOU RATHER...

...HAVE A PICNIC OUTSIDE OR EAT AT A RESTAURANT?

WOULD YOU RATHER...

...BE THE STRONGEST CHICKEN OR THE SLOWEST CHEETAH?

...HAVE ROLLER-SKATES OR A POGO STICK?

...EAT A DEAD BEETLE OR A LIVE CATERPILLAR?

WOULD YOU RATHER...

...HAVE FOUR ARMS OR FOUR LEGS?

WOULD YOU RATHER...

...DESIGN A NEW TOY OR DIRECT A MOVIE?

...HAVE TO SNEEZE EVERY 5 MINUTES OR BURP EVERY 2 MINUTES?

...BE A GROWN-UP RIGHT NOW OR STAY A KID FOREVER?

...FEEL ITCHY
EVERY DAY
OR
GET TICKLED
EVERY DAY?

...HAVE A ROBOT
TO PLAY GAMES WITH
OR
A ROBOT THAT
BRINGS
YOU FOOD?

...EAT EVERY MEAL WITH A SPOON OR A FORK?

...IT RAIN GLITTER OR APPLE JUICE?

WOULD YOU RATHER...

...BE ABLE TO CONTROL WHEN IT RAINS OR WHEN IT SNOWS?

WOULD YOU RATHER...

...HAVE TWO LONG FRONT TEETH LIKE A BEAVER OR NO TEETH AT ALL?

...EAT WET CAT FOOD OR DOG TREATS?

...HAVE EYES THAT GLOW IN THE DARK OR HAIR THAT GLOWS IN THE DARK?

WOULD YOU RATHER...

...LOOK LIKE A SKUNK OR SMELL LIKE A SKUNK?

WOULD YOU RATHER...

...STEP IN PEE IN THE BATHROOM OR SIT ON A POOP-SMEARED TOILET?

WOULD YOU RATHER...

...HAVE A BABY PUKE ON YOU OR PEE ON YOU?

WOULD YOU RATHER...

...BE ABLE TO SPEAK EVERY LANGUAGE ON EARTH OR TALK TO ALIENS?

...HAVE TO YELL EVERYTHING YOU NEED TO SAY OR RUN EVERYWHERE YOU NEED TO GO?

...BE A FRIENDLY GHOST OR A SCARY MONSTER?

...DRINK A SMOOTHIE MADE OF CRUSHED LADYBUGS
OR
EAT 5 LIVE SNAILS?

...LIVE WHERE YOU ARE FOREVER
OR
MOVE TO ANOTHER COUNTRY?

WOULD YOU RATHER...

...GO TO
A WIZARD SCHOOL
OR
TO A SUPERHERO
SCHOOL?

WOULD YOU RATHER...

...MEET YOUR FAVORITE
MOVIE STAR
OR
THE PRESIDENT
OF THE UNITED STATES?

WOULD YOU RATHER...

...BE ABLE TO BREATHE UNDERWATER OR WALK ON WATER?

WOULD YOU RATHER...

...LIVE ON A FARM OR LIVE IN THE CITY?

...SMELL BAD
OR
HAVE WALRUS
TEETH?

...NEVER HAVE
TO BRUSH
YOUR TEETH AGAIN
OR
NEVER HAVE
TO BATHE AGAIN?

...HUG A SLIMY EEL
OR
A PRICKLY
PORCUPINE?

...HAVE TO CRAWL
ON ALL FOURS
OR
ONLY BE ABLE
TO WALK
BACKWARDS?

WOULD YOU RATHER...

...LICK THE BOTTOM OF YOUR SHOE
OR
EAT YOUR BOOGERS?

WOULD YOU RATHER...

...TURN INTO A PUPPY EVERY TIME YOU EAT
OR
TURN INTO A KITTEN EVERY TIME YOU DRINK?

WOULD YOU RATHER...

...DRINK A GLASS OF SWEAT OR A GLASS OF DROOL?

WOULD YOU RATHER...

...HAVE TOOTHPASTE THAT SMELLS LIKE DOG FARTS OR TASTES LIKE SOUR MILK?

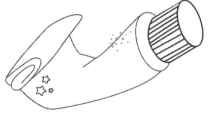

WOULD YOU RATHER...

...HAVE THE POWER TO FREEZE TIME OR GO BACK IN TIME?

WOULD YOU RATHER...

...HAVE TO POOP 12 TIMES A DAY OR HAVE DIARRHEA EVERY TIME YOU POOP?

WOULD YOU RATHER...

...HAVE SUPER SPEED OR THE ABILITY TO CHANGE INTO ANIMALS?

WOULD YOU RATHER...

...RIDE A HIPPO TO SCHOOL OR A CAMEL?

WOULD YOU RATHER...

...HAVE
10 WARTS
OR
10 BLISTERS?

WOULD YOU RATHER...

...PEE YOUR PANTS
EVERY DAY
OR
TELL EVERYONE
AROUND YOU WHEN
YOU HAVE TO FART?

WOULD YOU RATHER...

...BE A MAGICAL WIZARD OR A SUPERHERO?

WOULD YOU RATHER...

...FART SUPER LOUD OR POOP YOUR PANTS SILENTLY?

WOULD YOU RATHER...

...BE
AN ASTRONAUT
OR
A FIRE FIGHTER?

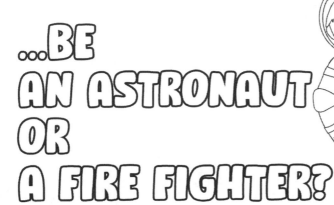

WOULD YOU RATHER...

...EAT
VINEGAR-FLAVORED
MUFFINS
OR
EGG-FLAVORED
ICE CREAM?

WOULD YOU RATHER...

...LET SOMEONE SPIT IN YOUR EYEBALL OR SPIT IN YOUR MOUTH?

WOULD YOU RATHER...

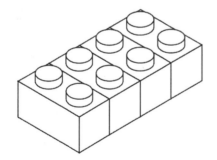

...STEP ON A LEGO OR STEP IN A PUDDLE WEARING SOCKS?

...HAVE A GIANT TONGUE OR GIANT TOES?

WOULD YOU RATHER...

...WRESTLE A CAT-SIZED GORILLA OR A BEAR-SIZED SQUID?

WOULD YOU RATHER...

...DRINK A CUP OF SOUR MILK OR EAT A ROTTEN POTATO?

WOULD YOU RATHER...

...LIVE IN A HOUSE FULL OF CHEESE OR JELLO?

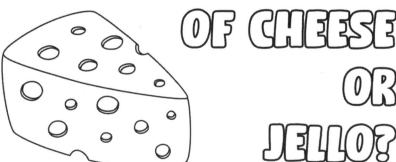

WOULD YOU RATHER...

...SNEEZE BACON OR HAVE KETCHUP FLAVORED TEARS?

WOULD YOU RATHER...

...USE A LITTER BOX TO GO TO THE BATHROOM OR BE WALKED LIKE A DOG?

...HAVE A PIG'S
NOSE
OR
A BIRD'S BEAK?

...HAVE A PET ANT
THAT CAN ONLY TELL
KNOCK-KNOCK JOKES
OR
A TALKING DUCK
THAT BITES?

WOULD YOU RATHER...

...BE
THE HERO
OR
THE SIDEKICK?

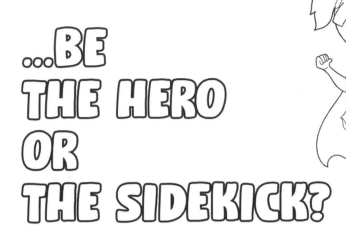

WOULD YOU RATHER...

...HAVE A BOOGER
HANGING
FROM YOUR NOSE
OR
A PIECE OF BROCCOLI
STUCK BETWEEN
YOUR TWO FRONT TEETH?

WOULD YOU RATHER...

...USE YOUR TONGUE TO WASH ALL YOUR CLOTHES OR ALL YOUR DISHES?

WOULD YOU RATHER...

...HAVE TWO NOSES OR TWO MOUTHS?

WOULD YOU RATHER...

...HAVE A HEAD THE SIZE OF A GRAPE
OR
THE SIZE
OF A WATERMELON?

WOULD YOU RATHER...

...EAT 2 OF YOUR OWN TURDS
OR
EAT 1 OF YOUR FRIEND'S TURDS?

WOULD YOU RATHER...

...EXPLORE THE OCEAN FOR DOLPHINS
OR
EXPLORE THE JUNGLE FOR GORILLAS?

WOULD YOU RATHER...

...SHOW UP TO SCHOOL ON THE BACK OF A DINOSAUR
OR
IN A RACE CAR?

Made in the USA
Columbia, SC
04 December 2020

26355924R00063